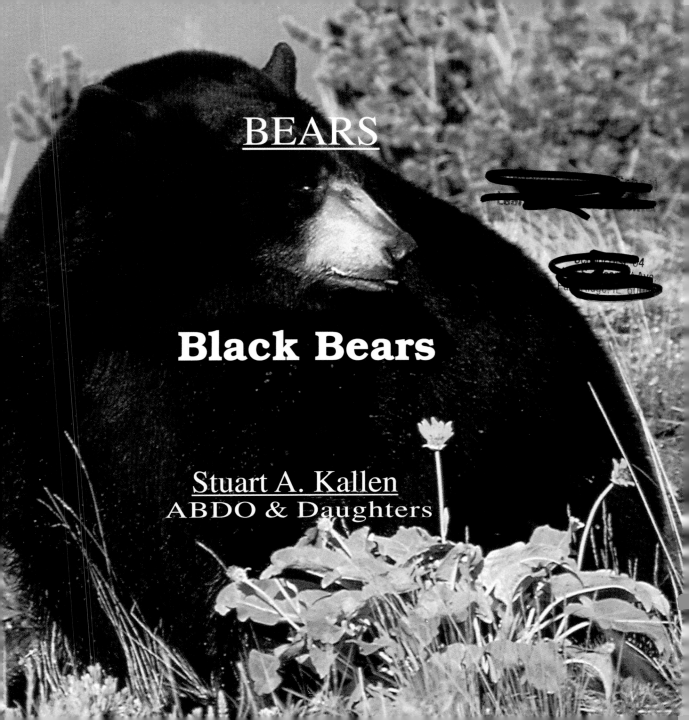

BEARS

Black Bears

Stuart A. Kallen
ABDO & Daughters

visit us at
www.abdopub.com

Published by Abdo & Daughters, 4940 Viking Drive, Suite 622, Edina, Minnesota 55435.

Printed in the United States.

Cover Photo credits: Peter Arnold, Inc.
Interior Photo credits: Peter Arnold, Inc.

Edited by Lori Kinstad Pupeza

Library of Congress Cataloging-in-Publication Data

Kallen, Stuart A., 1955-
      Black bears / Stuart A. Kallen.
      p.   cm. -- (Bears)
      Includes index
      Summary: Briefly describes the physical characteristics, habitat, and behavior of black bears.
      ISBN 1-56239-590-4
      1. Black bear--Juvenile literature. [1. Black bear. 2. Bears]
      I. Title. II. Series: Kallen, Stuart A., 1955- Bears.
      QL737.C27K34   1998
      599.74'446--dc20   95-52343
                                      CIP
                                      AC

Contents

Black Bears and Their Family

Black bears are **mammals**. Like humans, they breathe air with lungs, are **warm blooded**, and **nurse** their young with milk.

Bears first **evolved** around 40 million years ago. They were small, meat-eating, tree-climbing animals. The early bears were related to coyotes, wolves, foxes, raccoons, and even dogs. Today, there are eight different **species** of bears. They live in 50 countries on three **continents**.

The scientific name for the black bear is *Ursus americanus*. These are Latin words. *Ursus* means "bear." *Americanus* means "American." The black bear is the American bear!

Black bears are the most common type of bear in the world, numbering about 700,000.

Size, Shape, and Color

Black bears are the smallest bears in North America. The average adult is 35 to 40 inches (89 to 102 cm) when standing on all four feet. Black bears are about 4.5 to 6 feet (1.3 to 1.8 m) when standing up on their hind legs. A black bear can weigh from 125 to 600 pounds (57 to 272 kg).

Black bears have heavily built bodies with short legs, necks, and tails. They have large heads with rounded ears. Their eyes are small for so large an animal.

Black bears have large, pointed teeth that help them catch and kill **prey**. They can stand up easily on their large, wide feet. Each toe ends in a long, curving claw.

Most black bears have black coats with brown eyes and brown **muzzles**. Black bears have been seen in many colors, including cinnamon, beige, blue, and even white.

Opposite page: A black bear eating birch bark.

Where They Live

Black bears are the most common bears in North America. They live in areas where there are dense forests. Black bears live in 42 states in America, and 11 of the 12 Canadian **provinces**. They live in northern Mexico, the Rocky Mountains, Canada, and the lower **Arctic Circle**.

Visitors to America's national parks often see black bears. The bears have been spotted walking down roads, raiding picnic baskets, and digging through trash cans.

Black bears are most plentiful in the vast forests of the Pacific Northwest. There are also many black bears in the mixed hardwood forests of the eastern United States and Canada.

Canada

United States

Mexico

Black bears may also be found in the northern Great Lakes states of Minnesota, Wisconsin, and Michigan.

A black bear in Montana.

Senses

Bears are very smart animals that learn quickly. They are curious and have very good memories. Because of their small eyes, there is a myth that bears cannot see well. But bears have good eyesight. They can tell the difference between colors, and see well at night. They can spot moving objects at a far distance. Bears stand on their hind legs to be able to see farther.

Bears see and hear well, but their sense of smell is their most important sense. Their keen sense of smell allows them to find mates, avoid humans, locate their **cubs**, and gather food. Bears have been known to detect a human scent 14 hours after a person has passed along a trail. Experiments have proven that bears can smell food three miles (4.8 km) away!

Opposite page: A black bear seated in a tree lets out a yawn.

Defense

Bears are very strong. They move rocks and large logs with one paw. No animal of an equal size is as powerful as a bear. A black bear may kill a moose, elk, or deer with a single blow to the neck. Black bears have 20 long claws and can easily rip the bark off trees.

Bears are careful of anything that comes near them. Bears attack for two reasons—to get food and to defend themselves. When hunting large game, bears may stalk it like a cat. There is a myth that bears are slow. But they are surprisingly quick. A black bear can easily run 35 to 40 mph (56-64 kmph) for short distances.

Most black bears would rather run away from a human than attack. Bears attack when protecting their young, if their escape route is blocked, if they are protecting food sources, or if they are startled.

Black bears can be fierce when protecting their young.

Food

Bears eat just about anything. They will eat tiny insects like grasshoppers or giant creatures like moose. Bears also eat fish, fruit, berries, nuts, acorns, and roots. What they eat depends on the time of year.

Black bears are not the greatest hunters. Eighty-five percent of their diet is made up of vegetables. Black bears live in forests that are dotted with meadows. This provides them with different kinds of berries and other foods. Black bears will strip the bark from trees to lick the sweet sap underneath.

Cabins, camps, garbage cans, and town dumps are often raided by bears looking for an easy meal. To get to food, a black bear will rip down the wall of a cabin or jump on a car roof until the doors pop open! Once bears get a taste for human food, they are hard to stop. Never, ever feed a bear.

Opposite page: A black bear feeding on leaves in the Great Smoky Mountains.

Bear Hibernation

As summer ends, black bears become very fat. They eat so much they gain 30 pounds (14 kg) a week! They need to store this fat to get them through the long, cold winter.

As winter comes, black bears find a cave or hollow log to move into. This is called a **den**. The dens are hidden and secure.

By mid-October and early November the bears are fast asleep—**hibernating**—in their dens. When the snows come and temperatures drop well below freezing, the bear is in a deep sleep.

When spring comes the bears wake up. They yawn, stretch, and limp out of the den, weighing only half as much. Female bears will have **cubs** that were born at the end of the hibernation. The bears are hungry and thirsty. The bears continue to lose

weight for a few months until summer comes and
food is once again plentiful.

A black bear in its den at the end of hibernation.

Babies

Bears usually mate in May and June. Female bears are pregnant for about eight months. **Cubs** are born in January or February while the mother is sleeping in the **den**.

Usually two cubs are born, but some bears may have as many as four. The cubs are very tiny, and weigh between 8.5 and 11.5 ounces (240 to 330 g). They are blind, bald, and helpless.

By the time they are five weeks old, they learn to walk. By springtime, cubs are ready to leave the den. The first few months outside the den are tough for baby black bears. Cubs may be killed by eagles, bobcats, or mountain lions.

By the time they are 6 months old, bear cubs weigh 55 to 65 pounds (25 to 30 kg). The cubs will spend another winter in the den with their mother.

After one year, the mother will force them to go out on their own. Young bears have a tough time. Larger male bears chase them. With their lack of experience, they are often drawn to garbage dumps for food scraps.

These cubs are having fun climbing a tree.

Black Bear Facts

Scientific Name: *Ursus americanus.*

Average Size: 35 to 40 inches (89 to 102 cm) when standing on all 4 feet—4.5 to 6 feet (1.3 to 1.8 m) tall when standing up.

125 to 600 pounds (57 to 272 kg). Males are about one-third larger than females.

Where They're Found: 42 of the 50 states in the United States; 11 of the 12 Canadian **provinces** from Newfoundland to British Columbia; the lower **Arctic Circle**; the wooded Sierra Madre Mountains of Mexico.

Glossary

Arctic Circle - the very cold region near the North Pole.

continent (KAHN-tih-nent) - one of the seven main land masses: Europe, Asia, Africa, North America, South America, Australia, and Antarctica. Black bears are found only in North America.

cub - a baby bear.

den - a cave, hole in the ground, or hole in a tree used by a bear for a shelter.

evolve - for a species to develop or change over millions of years.

hibernate - to spend the winter in a deep sleep.

mammal - a class of animals, including humans, that have hair and feed milk to their young.

muzzle - the nose, mouth, and jaws of an animal.

nurse - to feed a young animal or child milk from the mother's breast.

prey - an animal hunted and captured for food.

province - a division of a country like a state. Canada is divided into 12 provinces.

species (SPEE-sees) - a group of related living things that have the same basic characteristics.

warm blooded - an animal whose body temperature remains the same and warmer than the outside air or temperature.

Index

T-14301